CN00686942

To a Good Friend

To
Marion

love
Marion.

To a Good Friend

A *Heartwarmers*™
Gift Book
WPL

To a Good Friend
A Heartwarmers™ Gift Book
©WPL 2002
Text by Anne Dodds
Illustration by Jo Parry - Advocate

Printed in China
Published by WPL 2002

ISBN 1-904264-07-7

For information on other Heartwarmers™ gift books,
gifts and greetings cards, please contact
WPL
14 Victoria Ind. Est. Wales Farm Road
London W3 6UU UK
Tel: +44 (0) 208 993 7268 Fax: +44 (0) 208 993 8041
email: wpl@atlas.co.uk

I hope you'll like this little book
which is especially for you,
and I wish you luck and happiness
in everything you do.

Your friendship means the world to me
and I just want you to know,
I'll always feel close to you
wherever I may go.

It's because we share a special bond
that distance can't erase,
and I always feel my spirits lift
when I see your smiling face.

I just can't help but wonder
what life would be like today,
if you and I had never met
and simply gone another way.

When I think of all the occasions
when you've been there to see me through,
it makes me wonder how on earth
I could manage without you.

Because words alone
can not convey
just how lost
I would be,
if I didn't have
such a good friend
always looking out for me.

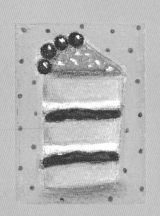

We've shared so many happy times
when we've laughed until we've cried,
and we've also shared some sad times
when both of us have tried...

...to just be there for each other
with a reassuring smile,
to give a helping hand when needed
or to simply talk a while.

Whatever happens in my life
I know I can come to you,
and the welcome I'll receive
will help to see me through.

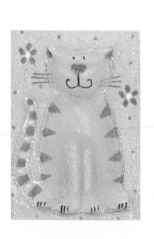

I know you'll always be there
at any time of day,
to listen and to understand
in your own special way.

You'll be supportive
and cheerful,
you'll be optimistic too,
so that by the time I've left
I'll find my grey skies
have turned blue.

Simply knowing that you're my friend
always makes me smile,
for it's special people just like you
who make life so worthwhile.

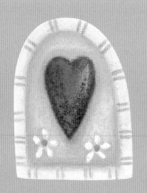

If I were asked the reasons why
you mean so much to me,
I wouldn't know just where to start
there are such a lot you see.

Maybe it's your patience,
the way you always try
to understand my problems
and to help me reason why.

Or could it be that so often
you can see the funny side of things,
which helps me cope more easily
with the setbacks that life brings.

Your brilliant sense of humour
and your wonderful sense of fun,
can instantly chase the gloom away
and welcome back the sun.

It really means a lot to me
that I can count on you,
to help me see more clearly
by giving your caring point of view.

Your loyalty means more to me
with every passing day,
it's how I know that we'll be friends
forever, come what may.

I don't know if I've told you
how glad I'll always be,
that the path you chose was destined
to lead you straight to me.

For I'll always feel so lucky
that I have someone like you,
to share a special friendship
that will last our whole lives through.

To be there standing by me
when others let me down,
always trying to cheer me up
when you see me with a frown.

To be so happy for me
when things are going great,
and to always be among the first
to help me celebrate.

The happy times I spend with you
mean so much to me,
we get along so well
and I just love your company.

Today and every single day
I hope in your heart you know,
I will never let you down
because I care about you so.

I'll be there when you need me
and I will always try,
to help in any way I can
without asking why.

It makes me
very happy
if I can play a part
in helping you
to smile again,
bringing joy back
to your heart.

Your friendship's important to me
it helps me every day,
to find the courage and the confidence
to do things my own way.

I'm happy in the knowledge
I have a friend who cares,
someone I can always trust
anytime and anywhere.

We try to keep an open mind
when we don't see eye to eye,
and resolve our differences
before we say goodbye.

We both know the importance
of seeing another's point of view,
and we always listen to each other
before deciding what to do.

For you and I will never let
a disagreement spoil our day,
life's too short and we care too much
to have it any other way.

As time goes by, our friendship
just grows stronger day by day,
and that makes me happier
than any words can say.

You are such a good friend
and my favourite confidante too,
and I know whatever happens
I can always depend on you.

So I'll always
feel so lucky
that the paths
we chose that day,
led us to each other
and not some other way.

Because friendship is a precious gift
and I know my whole life through,
I'll always be so grateful
that I have a friend like you.

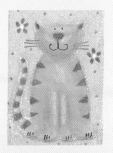

A Heartwarmers™
Gift Book

WPL

Also available from Heartwarmers™

Thank you Mum

For a Special Friend

For my Sister

For You Mum

100 Reasons why I Love You

For my Husband

Believe in Yourself

For my Nan

I Love You Because...

For a Special Daughter

For a Special Mum